Norwegiar
The Surv

1st edition published in September 2025

Published by Skapago Publishing Werner Skalla, Von-Müller-Str. 12, 93437 Furth im Wald, Germany, info@skapago.eu.

Picture credits:
All photos and illustrations © Daniela Skalla except:
p. 23 © Max Skalla
Cover designed by Max Skalla

ISBN: 978-3-945174-37-1

Norwegian Grammar: The Survival Guide

Werner Skalla

Skapago Publishing
www.skapago.eu

Contents

Is grammar overrated? Yes and no.

Don't get me wrong – I'm *not* saying grammar is *not* important.
Yes, you will have to learn your irregular verbs. By heart. It will hurt, and there is no way around it (if you know one, publish it and get rich by doing so).
Yes, people will misunderstand you if you make major grammar mistakes.
Yes, some mistakes will make you sound weird.

But that does not mean you need to know everything you find in a 300+ pages Norwegian grammar book before you start speaking.

Because – this is **one of the biggest mistakes** language learners make: they wait for the perfect moment to start speaking since they are afraid of making mistakes. The problem is: this moment will never come. I don't want to scare you, but in all languages (also in Norwegian) grammar is so complicated that it is impossible *not* to make mistakes.

I don't want to be one of those teachers who throw cheap phrases at you like "Embrace your mistakes! Leave your comfort zone! If you are afraid of speaking, start speaking! Just do it!"

I know it's not that easy. If you are afraid of making mistakes, then you are afraid of making mistakes, and the "just do it!" encouragements are useless.

My suggestion: if you are afraid of speaking Norwegian because of mistakes, then take some time and learn just the **ten vitally important grammar items** from this guide. You can "fill up" with the rest later.
So this is the purpose of this guide: you'll find a *structure* separating the vitally important grammar from the not-so-important stuff (fortunately, that's most of grammar).

By the way, before I tell you the principle of how I group the grammar topics, let me state one more thing (many language teachers will kill me for saying this, but I'll do it all the same. Don't tell them where I live please):

Pronunciation is more important than grammar.

I am always shocked at how bad pronunciation training is at most traditional language schools, including universities (shame on them). It is scientifically proven that more misunderstandings happen because of bad pronunciation than because of bad grammar. And when people want to say that someone is bad at a certain language, they say "he has an accent", not "he lacks grammar skills".
So if you are ready to upgrade your pronunciation, check out my free email mini-course on pronunciation:

But now, back to grammar. I will use a traffic light system:

Red grammar

Things you MUST know. Otherwise nobody will understand you and/or you will sound like an idiot.

Yellow grammar

Nice to have. You will sound more natural. Learn it if you have time. No big problem if you get it wrong though.

Green grammar

Everything else. If you want to be really good or pass an exam, learn that too. However, if you make mistakes with this in spoken Norwegian, native speakers will barely notice.

Before I present the actual red grammar and yellow grammar topics to you, let me clarify a few common questions:

- **Why do Norwegian courses (even my own course) present yellow and green grammar early on?**

Because this guide is about what you should know *actively*, i.e. when you are *speaking*. To know how the Norwegian language works, you will also have to learn the yellow and green stuff. I don't believe in methods that "hide" grammar from you because they don't want to scare you. You're a grown-up, aren't you? So why are you afraid of several tenses? Read through the explanations in your textbook so that you understand the structure and function of the Norwegian language. But to make yourself *understood* in Norwegian, the red stuff will do.

- **Isn't this a question of level? Doesn't an advanced student at B2 level need to know more grammar than an A1 student?**

Yes and no. Obviously, if you want to pass an exam where a certain level requires certain grammar topics, you will have to know all the required grammar. But in everyday life you don't tell your Norwegian friends "I don't know how to say what I did yesterday because I'm just on level A1 – wait until I have finished my A2". You want some practical, easy way of expressing yourself.

Obviously at an advanced level you want to get more sophisticated stuff right. But I see students at all levels, even super advanced students, who (for example) occasionally mix up genders. Still, this is no problem at all for being understood.

This gender problem is a good example for what I want to say here: if I did not explain genders to you in chapter 2 of my Norwegian course, you would constantly be asking "why do they sometimes say **en** and sometimes **ei** and sometimes **et**?" I need to explain that early on so that you *see how things work* in Norwegian. But that does not mean that you need to avoid mistakes with this topic at all costs.

- **Does that mean I should *not* learn the yellow/green grammar?**

No. Of course you should learn it. For example, if you don't start learning the genders with their noun right away (e.g. **en gutt**, but **et barn**), how do you expect you will ever get this right at a higher level? I'm saying that for the yellow/green grammar *mistakes don't hurt* (a lot). But when it comes to the red grammar, a misunderstanding is almost guaranteed. This guide is made to help you understand what you MUST learn so that you can get along in spoken Norwegian.

So without further ado, let's start.

Red grammar

Verbs and pronouns

jeg	I
du	you (*one person*)
han	he
hun	she
den/det	it
vi	we
dere	you (*several persons*)
de	they

- A *verb* is a word that tells you what someone does: ***eat, sleep, work, fly, love*** ... these are all verbs.
- A *pronoun* is a word that replaces a person or a thing: ***I, you, he, she*** ...
- When we combine pronouns and verbs, we basically only allow certain endings, e.g. ***I drink*** – ***he drinks***.

But in Norwegian, things are easier! We have only one form for each verb and each tense. So regardless of who does what, we always use the same form for the verb.

In the present tense, this form usually ends with an **-r**.

Norwegian has two ways of saying ***you***: for one person you say **du** – for several persons you say **dere**.

When we talk about people, we use **han** for male and **hun** for female. Of course we can talk about things, too, but in Norwegian *even things have a gender* (see page 21)!

Therefore, we have two different words for the English ***it***:

- We use **den** for feminine and masculine things.
  Susanne vil ha en telefon. Den koster mye.

- We use **det** for neuter things.
  Susanne vil ha et rundstykke. Det koster ikke mye.

However it's not a big deal to mix up **det** and **den** if you do not know the gender of a noun (this is definitely not a red grammar issue).

Sometimes we don't know which word ***it*** is actually referring to. Then again, we do not know the gender of this thing either. In this case we use **det**: For example ***it rains*** (what is ***it*** referring to here? We have no idea ...) translates to Norwegian **det regner**.

Pronouns: subjects / objects

Subjects are the persons (or things) that are doing something. Every Norwegian sentence must have a subject.
Sentences can also have one (or more) *objects*. An object is a person (or thing) that is not doing anything in particular but is somehow the "victim" of the action that is being done by the subject.

This might sound a bit confusing, but consider how much this helps in avoiding a misunderstanding:
He likes her is definitely different from ***she likes him***.

Han liker henne.

Hun liker ham.

Imagine the following sentence:

Susanne henter Nils.

Obviously Susanne is doing something (she gets Nils), while Nils remains passive (he gets collected) – so Susanne is the subject and Nils is the object.

We can use *pronouns* for the subject and for the object. But the form of the pronoun often changes when the pronoun stands for an object. Look:

SUBJECT	OBJECT
jeg	meg
du	deg
han	ham (han)
hun	henne
den	den
det	det
vi	oss
dere	dere
de	dem
	seg

- Pay attention to the difference between **seg** and **ham/henne/dem**:
  ham/henne/dem = another person
  seg = him-/herself/themselves

Han ser seg.

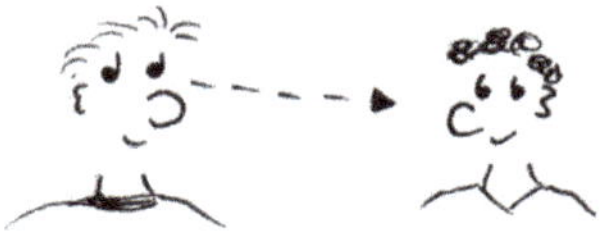

Han ser ham.

- Instead of **ham** you can also use **han**.
- Remember that ***you*** has three different translations in Norwegian:
  du, deg, dere:

  Where are you, Tom?
  → *Hvor er du, Tom?*

  I want to talk to you, Tom.
  → *Jeg vil snakke med deg, Tom.*

  Where are you, Tom and Betty?
  → *Hvor er dere, Tom og Betty?*

  I want to talk to you, Tom and Betty.
  → *Jeg vil snakke med dere, Tom og Betty.*

Questions

We have two types of questions. Let's start with the ones where you can answer ***yes*** or ***no***.
In these questions, the verb comes first.

Får jeg en gave også? → Ja. / Nei.

Verb

In questions with question words, we have the question word first (pretty logical, isn't it?).

Hva **er** det?

Verb
Question word

Numbers

0	null	
1	en/ei/ett (masculine/feminine/neuter)	
2	to	
3	tre	
4	fire	
5	fem	
6	seks	
7	sju	
8	åtte	
9	ni	
10	ti	
11	elleve	[ellve]
12	tolv	[tåll]
13	tretten	
14	fjorten	
15	femten	
16	seksten	[sæjsten]
17	sytten	[søtten]
18	atten	Remember: **atten** = 18, **åtti** = 80
19	nitten	
20	tjue	
21	tjueen	
22	tjueto	
30	tretti	
31	trettien	
40	førti	
50	femti	
60	seksti	
70	sytti	[søtti]
80	åtti	
90	nitti	
100	(ett) hundre	
101	(ett) hundreogen	
143	(ett) hundreogførtitre	
200	tohundre	
1000	(ett) tusen	
1015	(ett) tusenogfemten	
5130	femtusenetthundreogtretti	
1 000 000	en million	

Owning things (and people)

Of course we have the little words ***my***, ***your*** and so on in Norwegian, too (they are called *possessive pronouns*, by the way). But you do remember that we also have genders, right? That means if something belongs to me, I will use different words depending on the gender of that thing, or if I am talking about several things. However, for red grammar purposes, I solemnly allow you to mix up all the genders. **Min** will do, though it's great if you know **mitt** and **mine**, too.

min **sønn**

din **sønn**

hans **sønn**

hennes **sønn**

Belonging to someone

broren til Susanne

Use the word **til** to make it clear that this is Susanne's brother. Well, actually he doesn't really *belong* to her, but you know what I mean.

You can use this construction both for persons and things (so e.g. **bordet til Susanne** works, too).

From one to many

to, tre, mange ... kopper

to, tre, mange ... dører

to, tre, mange ... vinduer

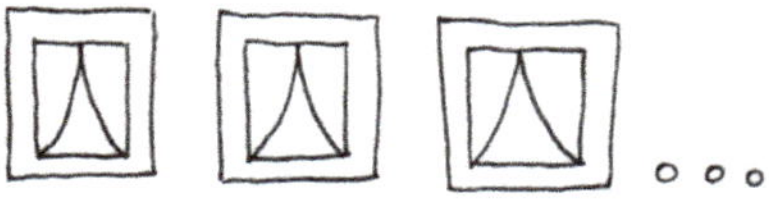

When we have several things/persons, we simply add an **-er** to Norwegian nouns.

If we already have an **-e** at the end, we don't add a second one:

en nisse → to nisser

Neuter words that are short (i.e. that have only one syllable) don't change, but that's actually yellow grammar:

et hus → to hus

Past tense (*preteritum*)

We are going to deal with *simple past* (in Norwegian: *preteritum*). There are more tenses, but one will do right now. Fortunately, in the *preteritum* we also have *only one single form* for each verb:

jeg gikk, du gikk, han gikk, vi gikk, dere gikk, de gikk

That was the good news – now for the bad news. How do you figure out what the *preteritum* form for a given verb is?
The verb may be *irregular* – then you don't figure it out at all, you just have to know it. There is a list of important irregular verbs on the next page.

The regular verbs have *4 possible endings*, and it can be a bit tricky to determine which is the right one, but if you mix them up, it's no problem:

ending –et: å våkne → jeg våknet
å arbeide → jeg arbeidet
(most verbs with two consonants/infinitive ending on -te/-de)
ending –te: å spise → jeg spiste
(most verbs with a single consonant)
ending –de: å leve → jeg levde
(most verbs with an infinitive ending on -ve, -eie)
ending –dde: å bo → jeg bodde
(most verbs ending on a vowel)

It might be a good idea to learn the *preteritum* for every single verb – even for the regular ones. In the word lists for my Norwegian textbook and my Norwegian online course, I will include the *preteritum* form.

However, once again, if you mix up the *preteritum* ending of regular verbs, it's no problem, though you should learn the irregular ones because you can get misunderstood if you don't get them right.

Important irregular verbs (present tense and *preteritum* forms)

infinitive	*present tense (if irregular)*	*preteritum*
å be		ba/bad
å bli		ble
å dra		dro/drog
å drikke		drakk
å drive		drev
å få		fikk
å finne		fant
å gå		gikk
å gi		ga/gav
å gjøre	gjør	gjorde
å ha		hadde
å hjelpe		hjalp
å kunne	kan	kunne
å legge		la
å ligge		lå
å måtte	må	måtte
å se		så
å selge		solgte
å sette		satte
å si		sa
å sitte		satt
å skrive		skrev/skreiv
å skulle	skal	skulle
å slå		slo
å spørre	spør	spurte
å stå		sto/stod
å ta		tok
å treffe		traff
å være	er	var
å ville	vil	ville
å vite	vet	visste

Comparing:
Harder, better, faster, stronger

Comparing things is not very difficult in Norwegian:

I Trondheim er det kaldere enn i Oslo.

All you do is add **-ere** to an adjective. Fortunately, the new form **kaldere** (we call that form the *comparative*) is the same for all genders and numbers:

Den er kaldere/det er kaldere/de er kaldere ...

Whenever there is a rule, there is an exception. Some adjectives cannot get an added **-ere**. Instead, they use the word **mer** in order to compare:

Min leilighet er mer moderne enn din leilighet.

The *superlative* is as easy as the *comparative*.
Instead of **-ere** (comparative), we use **-est:**

kald - kaldere - kaldest

For those adjectives that use **mer** in comparative, we use **mest** in superlative:

moderne - mer moderne - mest moderne

Unfortunately there are some irregural adjectives, too. You will have to learn them by heart. Sorry about that!

få	færre	færrest
bra/god	bedre	best
gammel	eldre	eldst
lang	lengre	lengst
lite(n)	mindre	minst
mange	flere	flest
mye	mer	mest
stor	større	størst
tung	tyngre	tyngst
ung	yngre	yngst
ille/ond/vond	verre	verst

That‘s it for the red grammar!

If you know the stuff you have learnt on the previous pages, you don‘t have any more excuses *not* to start speaking Norwegian.

If you are ready to get your Norwegian to the next level, please feel free to learn the yellow grammar on the next pages as well.

Genders

en  kopp → masculine

ei 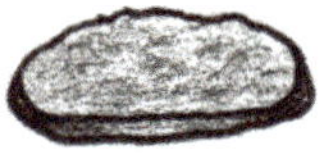 brødskive → feminine

et  rundstykke → neuter

As you can see, Norwegian cups are male, slices of bread are female and rolls are neutral. Sounds weird? Well, it is. But that's just the way this language works. So, in Norwegian we have three translations for the English word **a**:

en (for masculine people/things)
ei (for feminine people/things)
et (for neuter people/things)

That means: you cannot say ~~**et kopp**~~ – it's just wrong. It has to be **en kopp**, because cups are masculine.

How can you possibly know that a cup is masculine and not feminine or neuter? Unfortunately – you can't. You have to learn the gender of every single word by heart. Sorry! Perhaps you know this concept from another language, like German, French, Spanish, or Russian.

So if this has not been confusing enough, here is something else: Feminine Norwegian words (and *only* the feminine ones!) can also be masculine! So – you can say **en brødskive** instead of **ei brødskive**, but you cannot say ~~**ei kopp**~~ instead of **en kopp**.
Why is that so? My advice is best not ask. But, if you really, really want to know, you will have to read about Norwegian language history.

Definite article

In Norwegian we have no simple word for ***the***. Instead, we put the ***the*** at the end of the word it belongs to, as you can see in the following example:

a window → **et** vindu
the window → vindu**et**

If you come from a country where there is no difference between ***a window*** and ***the window*** (like Russia, Poland and so on), this might be a little complicated. Basically the difference here is as shown in the image: if we mean *any* window, we say **et vindu** (***a window***). If we are talking about a *certain* window (for example the only one in the room, or a window we have just mentioned before), we say **vinduet** (***the window***).

Next step: bear in mind that in Norwegian we have *genders*. That means that not only do we have three translations for the English ***a***, we also have three translations for the English ***the***. Again, the gender is linked to the word, so:

- neuter words end in **-et**
- masculine words end in **-en**
- feminine words end in **-a**

To make life a bit easier, you can treat female words the same as masculine words and give them an **-en** ending (but never the other way round).

Beware! For neuter words, the ending is **-et** but we do not pronounce the **-t**. We do not pronounce it at the end of the word **det** either. But the **t** is pronounced everywhere else in Norwegian!

et vindu
vinduet
en nisse
nissen
ei hånd
hånda

Adjectives

Adjectives are words that explain what things or persons are like (e.g. ***green, big, expensive, dark, possible*** ...).

We change adjectives

- according to the *gender* of the word they are describing
- according to the *number* of things (singular or plural, i.e. one or many)

en stor kopp
ei stor brødskive
et stort rundstykke
mange store kopper/brødskiver/rundstykker

One exception: Adjectives ending in **-ig** (**mulig, farlig, viktig** ...) cannot get a **-t** ending:

et hyggelig rom

There are some more exceptions, but these are green grammar items.

What you *should* learn however is that with adjectives, we also distinguish between the *indefinite* and the *definite* form.
Let's imagine a cup which is ***big***. In the indefinite form, we say:

en stor kopp

But now let's say it's not *any* cup, but a *certain* cup: the big cup.
In this case we say:

den store koppen

and for the other genders:

den store brødskiva
det store rundstykket

and for the plural:

de store koppene/brødskivene/rundstykkene

Notice two things:
1) The ending for the definite form is always **-e.** Simple!
2) In the definite form, the adjective doesn't want to be alone with the noun. Can you see that it's always together with **den** (for masculine and feminine nouns), **det** (for neuter nouns) and **de** (for plural)? We could say that these words would be the translation for the English ***the***. But that would not be 100% correct, since we translate ***the cup*** to **koppen** (and not **den koppen**), right? If you don't want to pass a translator's exam, you might find this discussion a bit too deep, but the point is this: whenever we use an adjective in the definite form, we also have to use the appropriate adjective article (that's the correct grammatical term for the words **den**, **det**, **de** in this context).

Once more, compare:

koppen <-> **den store koppen**

... whereas ~~**store koppen**~~ is wrong.

If you don't like the definite form, I still have some good news for you. Whenever the adjective comes *after* the word it is describing, it will be in the indefinite form. For example:

Den store kjelleren er mørk.
Det store rommet er mørkt.
De store rommene er mørke.

man

If we don't know who does something, we say **man**.

Man ser ei trang gate.

There is no really good English translation. You could say something like:

One can see a narrow street.

Notice that **man** does not have to be a man. Everybody is included, both men and women.

Two verbs in one sentence

Hun vil ikke vente.

Det kan hun se.

Jeg vil spise.

You learned about verbs in the red grammar section. When you have two verbs in one sentence, the second verb will be used in a form called the *infinitive,* which is the basic form of the verb, the one you would find in a dictionary, without any special ending.

If English is your first language, this might be confusing. The word ***wait*** is just the same in ***I wait*** and ***I have to wait***, isn't it? But replace ***I*** with ***she***, and you will see the difference:

she waits

she has to wait

This -s ending is actually the same as the Norwegian -r ending – except in Norwegian, we use it for all the personal pronouns, not only for ***he/she/it***.

Sentence structure

A Norwegian sentence is like a train. In every coach only certain pieces of information have booked a seat. The first coach is pretty open to almost everyone. However, the second coach is always reserved for the verb. Often in a sentence, there are a lot of other elements, but not every sentence has to have all of them. Some sentences have only what we call a *subject* (a person or a thing doing something) and a *verb* (the action that is being done). This is the minimum of what every Norwegian sentence must have.

Very often the subject is the first element in the sentence, but not necessarily. If it is not, it has to be in the third coach (after the verb) because the verb *must* be in the second coach! This is probably confusing for you if English is your first language.

Ok. But, actually, if we have *two verbs* – what about the second verb? Before I give you the answer, let me talk about two other coaches to our "sentence train".

The first one is *objects*. Well, actually, we have already discussed objects, haven't we? You learned about the words **meg**, **deg** and so on. We put them after the second verb (if there is one).

But there are still two coaches between the verbs. One of them contains the *subject*. As I said above, in many sentences (I would actually say, in most sentences) the subject comes before the first verb, in the grey coach. That means that the subject coach (right after the first verb) is then empty. The only time it gets occupied is when we start a sentence with something other than the subject. Behind the subject coach, we have another coach reserved for the *adverbial*. Now, what is that? I will give you some examples: **ikke**, **gjerne** and **egentlig**. Adverbials give a somewhat different meaning to the whole sentence. Look at **ikke**: it changes the meaning of the sentence 100%, doesn't it?

Jeg bor i Norge.
Jeg bor ikke i Norge.

Gjerne and **egentlig** do not necessarily change the meaning entirely, but still, they somehow modify the meaning of the sentence, or we could say, they give another "tone" to the meaning. And these words are placed *between the verbs*.

Ellers kan du egentlig ikke gjøre så mye galt.

Again, remember: we only *need* a subject and the first verb in a sentence, the other elements are not necessary, so they may or may not be there. If they are not, their coaches will simply remain empty.

Perfektum (present perfect)

Ok, you remember the *past tense*? There is also something similar to *present perfect* in Norwegian, called *perfektum*. It is going to be pretty easy since you already know *preteritum*.
Basically what you do is combine **har** + *perfektum*.
Now all you have to know is the *perfektum* form for each verb. First, the bad news: if the verb is irregular, you have to learn it by heart. Sorry. The forms are on page 30.
However, if the verb is regular, then it's very, very simple to get from *preteritum* to *perfektum*. All you do is take the *preteritum* form and remove the **-e** at the end. And when there is no **-e** at the end, like in **våknet**? Well, then you don't change anything at all. That's all there is to it!

ending –et: å våkne → jeg har våknet
ending –t: å spise → jeg har spist
ending –d: å leve → jeg har levd
ending –dd: å bo → jeg har bodd

Why do we actually need *perfektum* if we already have *preteritum*? The main rule here is: if the things that took place have some connection to the present, then we use *perfektum*.

Look at some examples from:

Erna har drukket to kopper kaffe.
→ Nå føler hun seg litt bedre.

Så here we use *perfektum* because Erna's coffee drinking in the past has an effect on the present (she is feeling better).

Hun har ikke spist ennå.

The connection to the present is not mentioned in the sentence, but obviously it is there: Erna would like to order some food, so the fact that she hasn't eaten yet describes her present situation.

This "connection to the present" can also mean that an action starting in the past is still going on:

Hun har alltid ventet.

... and she is still waiting.

Compare this to the situations where we use *preteritum*:

Susanne likte ikke gaven.

This happened on her birthday, but has no effect on the present.

Of course, sometimes (actually, pretty often), there can be quite some debate as to whether there is some relevance for the present or not. For example, look at the following sentence:

Det var en dum idé å gi henne gaven.

If Erna is just stating a fact, then *preteritum* is a good choice (no relevance for the present). But Erna might ask herself if she should have given Susanne another present. Then, *perfektum* would be a better choice.
But there is no need to turn it into a science. You will often hear Norwegians making the "wrong" choice, so let's not get too carried away, ok?

The only thing you should really remember is the following:

Ida og Per har vært gift i tre år.
Perfektum – they are still married.

Ida og Per var gift i tre år.
Preteritum – the marriage has ended.

To sum up, we use ...

Preteritum

- things that are over
- when we say at what time something happened

Perfektum

- things that are still going on
- things that have a connection to the present

Irregular verbs

To cheer you up a little, I include a photo of the traditional Norwegian *Hurtigruten* ship *Lofoten* near Molde, central Norway.

å be	har bedt
å bli	har blitt
å dra	har dratt
å drikke	har drukket
å drive	har drevet
å få	har fått
å finne	har funnet
å gå	har gått
å gi	har gitt
å gjøre	har gjort
å ha	har hatt
å hjelpe	har hjulpet
å kunne	har kunnet
å legge	har lagt
å ligge	har ligget
å måtte	har måttet
å se	har sett
å selge	har solgt
å sette	har satt
å si	har sagt
å sitte	har sittet
å skrive	har skrevet
å skulle	har skullet
å slå	har slått
å spørre	har spurt
å stå	har stått
å ta	har tatt
å treffe	har truffet
å være	har vært
å ville	har villet
å vite	har visst

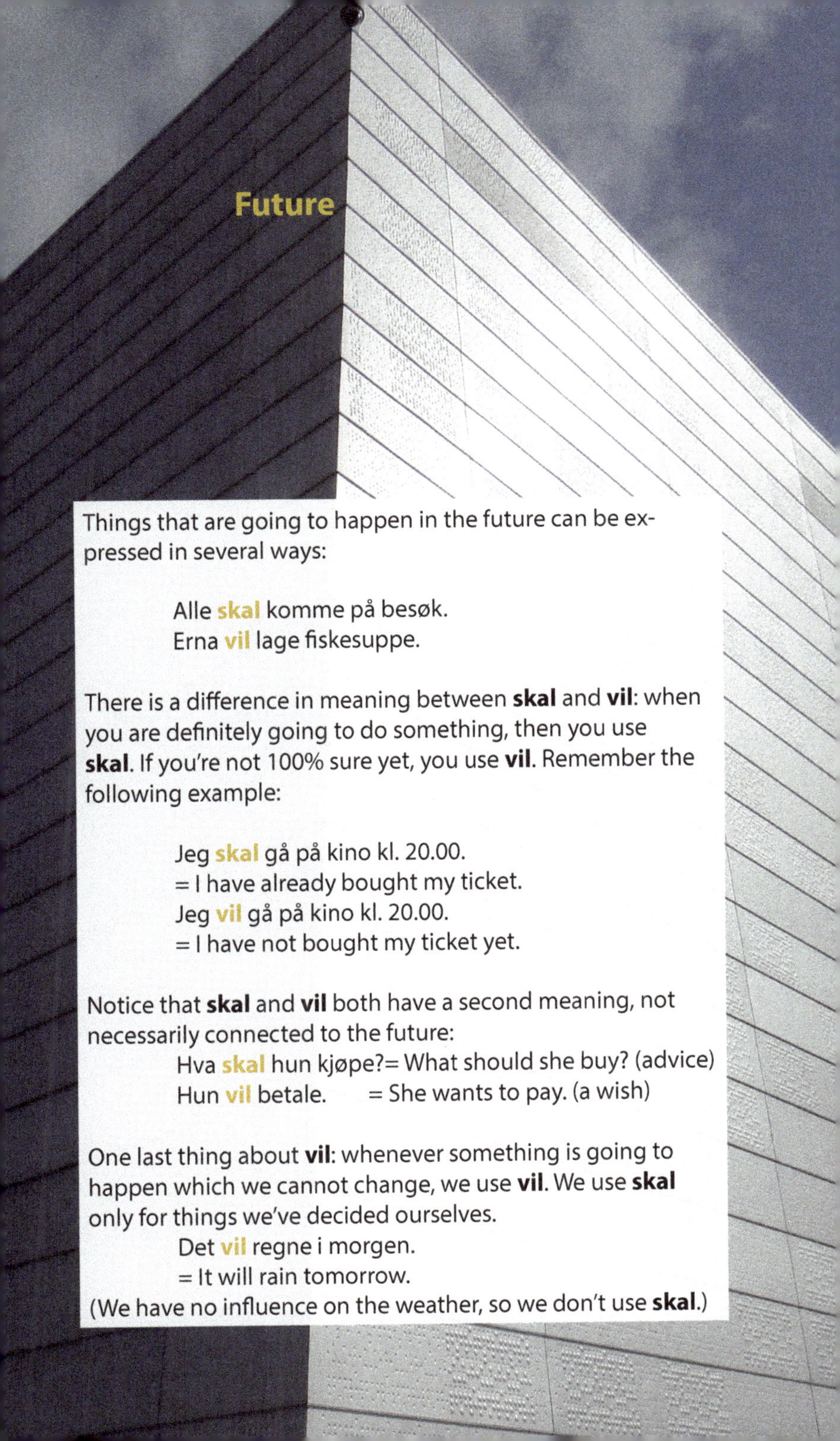

Future

Things that are going to happen in the future can be expressed in several ways:

> Alle **skal** komme på besøk.
> Erna **vil** lage fiskesuppe.

There is a difference in meaning between **skal** and **vil**: when you are definitely going to do something, then you use **skal**. If you're not 100% sure yet, you use **vil**. Remember the following example:

> Jeg **skal** gå på kino kl. 20.00.
> = I have already bought my ticket.
> Jeg **vil** gå på kino kl. 20.00.
> = I have not bought my ticket yet.

Notice that **skal** and **vil** both have a second meaning, not necessarily connected to the future:

> Hva **skal** hun kjøpe?= What should she buy? (advice)
> Hun **vil** betale. = She wants to pay. (a wish)

One last thing about **vil**: whenever something is going to happen which we cannot change, we use **vil**. We use **skal** only for things we've decided ourselves.

> Det **vil** regne i morgen.
> = It will rain tomorrow.

(We have no influence on the weather, so we don't use **skal**.)

Moving and not moving

These words have one thing in common: whenever we're moving, we use them in the left form (usually without an **-e** ending). When we're not moving, we use them in the right form.

Han **går** opp.	Han **er** oppe.
... ned	... nede
... inn	... inne
... ut	... ute
... hjem	... hjemme
... dit	... der
... hit	... her
... bort	... borte

Genders and their consequences

Genders are not only for nouns and adjectives. There are a few other words where you should take genders (and plural/singular) into consideration.

denne – dette – disse

These three words are the same as the English ***this***.

denne koppen
denne brødskiva
dette rundstykket
disse koppene/brødskivene/rundstykkene

Ok? Masculine + feminine, neuter, plural – the usual distribution. With all your Norwegian grammar experience, it's almost getting boring, isn't it?
Just a quick note! Notice that you always use the *definite form* of a noun (and an adjective, if you want to use one) after **denne/dette/disse**. Why? Pretty logical! When you say ***this***, you're never talking about just ***any*** person/thing, so it must be definite.

When we want to say ***this is ...*** we say **dette er ...** (we use the neuter form, even when the gender does not match the following noun):

Dette er en dusj.

noe(n)

When using these words alone they mean:

noe = something
noen = someone

Noen can also mean ***some*** when we combine it with nouns in the plural:

noen små øyer = some small islands

The final possible way of using **noe**:

noe undertøy = some underwear

What is the difference between **øyer** and **undertøy**?
(From a grammatical point of view, of course ...)
Well, **øyer** is a noun in the plural. I could also say **mange øyer**.
Undertøy is a noun in the singular that cannot be counted (also known as an uncountable noun). I could also say **mye undertøy** (see below).

mange – mye

When things are countable, in other words, we can count them, we use **mange**.
When things are uncountable, in other words, we cannot count them, we use **mye**. So:

mange øyer/venner/epler
mye undertøy/vann/snø

synes – tro

Boka er god, synes jeg. = Jeg har lest boka.
Boka er god, tror jeg. = Jeg har ikke lest boka.

We use **synes** when we express an opinion. However, we use **tro** when we want to say that we are not sure about a piece of information, i.e. when we ***think***, but ***don't know***.

kjenne – vite

Both words are translated as ***to know***, but they mean ***to know*** in two different ways. If you speak German, **å kjenne** means ***kennen***, **å vite** means ***wissen***.

Å kjenne means that you know who someone/something is:

Jeg kjenner Nils.

= I have seen him before, I know who he is.

Jeg kjenner Oslo.

= I know Oslo – I have been there before.

Å vite means you have knowledge of a certain fact:

Jeg vet hva han heter.

= I know what his name is.

Jeg vet ikke hvor han bor.

= I don't know where he lives.

Time

Klokka er 14.30.

14.20	→ **for** ti minutter siden
14.40	→ **om** ti minutter
fra kl. 14.20 til kl. 14.30	→ **i** ti minutter

Put that together with what you have learned about *preteritum* and *perfektum*:

Jeg har ventet på deg i ti minutter.
→ I started waiting at 14.20 and am still waiting.

Jeg ventet på deg i ti minutter.
→ I started waiting at, say, 14.15, and you came at 14.25.

enn/som

One more remark about comparing things. When there is a difference, use *comparative* and **enn**:

Oslo er større enn Bergen.
= Oslo is bigger than Bergen.

When there is no difference, then we use **like/så** and **som**:

Skien er like stor som Sarpsborg. /
Skien er så stor som Sarpsborg.
= Skien is as big as Sarpsborg.

Adverbs

Look at the following sentence:

Lise går raskt ut i gangen.

Why is there a **-t** ending on the word **raskt**?
Your first guess is probably that this is an adjective describing a neuter thing. But there is nothing neuter in this sentence: **Lise** is feminine (no doubt about that) and **gangen** is masculine. To find the answer to this mystery, I will ask you a question: what thing (or person) does **raskt** describe?
Certainly not **gangen**, and not **Lise** either: the sentence is not saying that Lise ***is*** quick, but it describes how she ***walks***. So **raskt** describes the verb **går**. Since it is not describing a thing or person, it is not an adjective. It is an *adverb* (easy to remember: *adverbs* describe *verbs* and *adjectives* describe *objects* and *subjects*).

Very often we can make adverbs out of adjectives. **Rask** is a good example. I can say:

en rask bil	a fast car	(adjective)
et raskt fly	a fast plane	(adjective)

But:

Lise går raskt.		(adverb)

So if we want to make an adverb from an adjective, we simply use the neuter form of that adjective (which generally, but not always, has a **-t** ending).

One last remark about this topic: there are no adverbs after **å være**. By definition, everything that explains what something ***is*** like, must be an adjective. Compare:

Susanne er rask.

Susanne går raskt.

Saying the date: ordinal numbers

For saying the date, you will have to learn *ordinal numbers* (e.g. ***first***, ***second***, and so on) – you can see them on the next page.

All the ordinal numbers printed in yellow are irregular, so you will have to learn them by heart. Sorry about that! But with the other ones, everything is easier. All you do is take the *cardinal number* (i.e. the "normal" number, like **femten**) and add a **-ende** [-enne] ending. If the number already has an **-e** ending, you will just add the **-nde**, and if it already has an **-en** ending, you will just add the **-de**.

1. første
2. andre
3. tredje
4. fjerde [fjære]
5. femte
6. sjette
7. sjuende
8. åttende
9. niende
10. tiende
11. ellevte
12. tolvte [tållte]
13. trettende
14. fjortende
15. femtende
16. sekstende [sæjs-]
17. syttende [søtt-]
18. attende
19. nittende
20. tjuende
21. tjueførste
22. tjueandre
30. trettiende

As you also can see we indicate the ordinal number with a little dot (***20th*** in English would be written as **20.** in Norwegian). Basically we use the definite article with ordinal numbers (pretty logical – usually it's ***the first*** and not ***a first***).

Ok, that was the first (and most difficult) step you have to take in order to say the date. The rest is easy. When we write the months, we use three letter abbreviations (e.g. **jan.** for **januar**), and the years are said in cardinal numbers (e.g. 2014 **totusenogfjorten**). Years before 2000 are said in two groups, e.g. 1981 **nitten åttien** (like 19 81), and some people do the same for years after 2000 (e.g. 2014 **tjue fjorten**). So for example:

05. okt. 2013 — den femte oktober totusenogtretten

If you like challenges, you can also say the month as an ordinal number. Then we put an **i** before the month:

05.10.2013 — den femte i tiende totusenogtretten

annen

Annen has two meanings: ***second*** and ***other***.

en annen mann
= another man
det andre huset til venstre
= the second house on the left

These are the forms for **annen**:

en annen kopp
ei anna dør
et annet vindu
mange andre kopper/dører/vinduer
den andre koppen/døra ...

Top question for grammar nerds!

Nå ser Nils noe helt annet.

Why do we use the neuter form **annet** here?

To answer this question, you must find out which word **annet** describes. Obviously this is **noe**. Since **noe** is neuter, we must use **annet**.

som

The word **som** connects two sentences. It replaces the subject or object that has been mentioned in the previous sentence.

Jeg ser **en film. Filmen** er helt fantastisk.
→ Jeg ser **en film som** er helt fantastisk.

In this example, **som** replaces the subject in the second sentence.

Den handler om **et land**. Jeg har lyst til å se **landet**.
→ Den handler om **et land som** jeg har lyst til å se.

In the second example, **som** replaces the object in the second sentence.

Leddsetninger
Subordinate clauses

I have told you again and again that the verb is in the second place in a sentence. I also told you that when there is a second verb, it has to be in the *infinitive* or *perfektum* form. Now look at the following sentence, and notice the verb **holder**:

Hun tror at det ikke holder med de to skjortene.

Holder is definitely not in the second place, and it is definitely in the present tense. So what has gone wrong here? You might say that there are two sentences – and you are totally right! There is:

Hun tror ...

and

... at det ikke holder med de to skjortene.

But still, look at the second sentence. Even if I ignore the word **at**, **holder** is definitely at place no. 3 and not at no. 2:

... (at) det	ikke	holder ...
1 (subj.)	2 (adv.)	3 (verb)

The reason for this special structure has to do with the word **at**. Take a look at this second sentence:

At det ikke holder med de to skjortene.

What does this sentence mean? Nothing at all! It has to be integrated into the first sentence starting with **Hun tror ...** Otherwise it just doesn't make sense. We call this type of sentences *subordinate clauses* (in Norwegian: *leddsetninger*). Subordinate clauses have two common characteristics:

1. They cannot stand alone.
2. They usually start with a word that integrates them into the main clause which in this case would be the word **at**. It could also be **som**, **hvis**, **når** ... We call these connecting words *subordinating conjunctions* (*subjunksjoner* in Norwegian). If you can't remember this name, that's fine with me, just remember that these connecting words must be present.

A common mistake many students make is that they think there is a main clause *and* a subordinate clause. This is a total misunderstanding. In reality there is a subordinate clause *within* a main clause. So in our example, the main clause is everything from **Hun** to **skjortene**, whereas the subordinate clause is the underlined part:

Hun tror <u>at det ikke holder med de to skjortene</u>.

Unfortunatly, we have reached the point where I have no choice but to inform you that subordinate clauses have a special sentence structure and the verb is *not* at the second place there. I'm sorry, but I wasn't the one who invented the Norwegian language!

Subordinate clauses always start with the *conjunction* (the word connecting them with the rest of the main clause). After that there is always the *subject*. Notice that we cannot put just any word at the beginning of the subordinate clause.
After the subject there is the *adverbial* (if there are any), e.g. **ikke**. And after that we have the *verb*. The rest of the sentence structure is exactly the same as in main clauses.
Obviously the big problem here is where to place the *adverbial*. Imagine that we delete the word **ikke** from the example:

Hun tror at det holder med de to skjortene.

We don't see a difference here between the structure in the main clause and in the subordinate clause, do we? So whenever you hear a connecting word (like **at**, **som** ...) and an adverbial (**ikke**, **ofte**, **allerede**, **egentlig** ...), then you should be aware that what you are dealing with may be a subordinate clause.

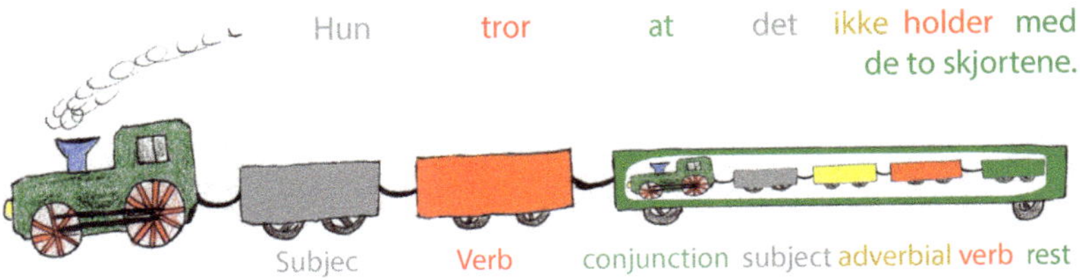

langt – lenge

Langt and **lenge** are *adverbs*. They come from the adjective **lang**.
There is a difference in meaning between the two: **langt** refers to distance, **lenge** refers to time.
But remember:

en lang vei (adjective)
ei lang tid (adjective)

Where to go from here

Now you have learned the key elements of the Norwegian grammar – I'm proud of you! You have no more excuses for why you cannot speak Norwegian.
Of course, a language is so much more than its grammar (as I said at the beginning, grammar is often overrated).

I'd love to help you to dive deeper into the Norwegian language. I know learning a language is hard work – that's why I believe we have to make the process fun!

Therefore I have created ***The Mystery of Nils*** – a Norwegian course based on a coherent **story** instead of boring dialogues.

The course will teach you everything about the **pronunciation, grammar, and vocabulary** and includes **more than 100 exercises** for listening comprehension, pronunciation and fluency. Check it out here: courses.skapago.eu/lp/norwegian

The essentials of the course are also available as a book. In fact, most grammar explanations in this guide are taken from the book.
You can download a free preview here:
www.skapago.eu/nils

Have fun learning Norwegian!

Would you like to learn **more languages?**

Skapago can help you even with other languages. What about learning **Chinese** with Jerry the horse, **Swedish** with Alfred the ghost or **German** with Jens and Jakob, the sparrows from Berlin?

More information:
www.skapago.eu

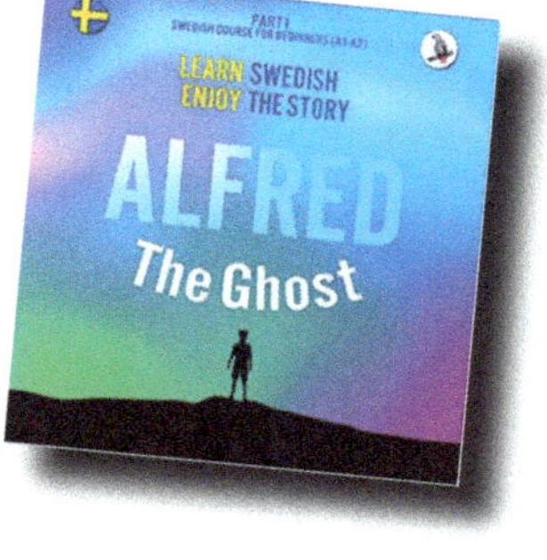

www.ingramcontent.com/pod-product-compliance
Ingram Content Group UK Ltd.
Pitfield, Milton Keynes, MK11 3LW, UK
UKHW061412310726
14168UKWH00032B/498

9 783945 174371